SHORE PATROLS   JEEPS   G.I. BRIDES   U.S.S. AUGUSTA   NISSEN HUTS   VICARAGE ROAD CAMP

United States Naval Advanced Amphibious Base Plymouth 1943-45

IDAHO WAY   CANDY   LITTLE AMERICA   MANADON HOSPITAL   CHRISTMAS PARTIES

Arthur L. Clamp

Queen Anne's Battery
This was the centre of operations for the amphibious force accommodated around Plymouth. This view shows where landing craft ships could be maintained and launched; there were three rail tracks laid down for carriage purposes and the Teat's Hill flats behind were occupied as the communication centre for all local operations.

This version of the book is virtually as originally published.
There are now additional pages at the back providing information about the author.

The republishing project is being managed by Arthur's grandson, Steven Gibson. We aim to find all the research that he was involved in publishing, preserving it for the next generation as part of 'The Clamp Collection'.

OPERATION OVERLORD: THE ASSAULT ON EUROPE

This booklet has been produced on the 50th anniversary year of the D Day landings which took place on 6th June, 1944, with troops from the Plymouth area landing on *Utah* beach on the Cherbourg peninsula.

There were five landing areas code named *Utah, Omaha, Gold, Juno* and *Sword*. The first two were undertaken by American forces based in the West Country and up to Poole in Dorset, the others by British and Commonwealth troops based around the Southampton area and up to Newhaven. All these troops were supported by considerable air cover and naval power from units stationed in various parts of Great Britain.

The landings have been described as the largest and most complex amphibious assaults in military history involving 13,000 aircraft, 3,500 gliders, 4,000 landing ships, 1,300 warships, 1,600 merchant ships with about 3½ million troops of which 1¼ million were American.

The United States Naval Amphibious Base at Plymouth was set up in November, 1943, and closed in September, 1945. Its main purpose was set up shore base facilities for the reception and training of troops in the various exercises which took place at Slapton during the first half of 1944, the smooth departure of 36,000 U.S. troops in late May and early June, 1944, and various post landing tasks such as supplying ammunition to bombarding ships along the French coast, the maintenance and repair of damage landing vessels and the receiving of casualties and displaced troops during the latter half of 1944.

On 15th December, 1942, the Admiralty informed C-in-C Plymouth that accommodating and berthing arrangements were required at Appledore for training, Falmouth for training and assault, Fowey for training, Plymouth for assault, Salcombe for training, Dartmouth for training and assault, and Teignmouth for training and were to be available by 1st July, 1943.

It can be seen from the map on page 11 that these bases were to be used by the U.S. 4th and 29th Infantry Divisions whose troops were stationed in Devon and Cornwall. Throughout the second half of 1943 and the first half of 1944 thousands of U.S. troops moved into Devon and Cornwall with thousands of vehicles and an almost countless array of equipment and provisions occupying hundreds of sites in both counties.

Plymouth and its surrounds, like other ports, virtually became a large encampment of American troops with its waterways mooring many vessels, its open spaces occupied by temporary tented camps, its roads and lanes lined with thousands of boxes of ammunition and parked and camouflaged military vehicles standing in readiness for the invasion of France. There were restrictions on the movement of civilians, a total blackout of information yet it soon became apparent to Plymothians that something was about to take place.

Some 36,000 troops left Plymouth in two waves. The first was Force U (for Utah) made up of troops from Brixham, Dartmouth, Salcombe and Plymouth comprising 865 ships leaving from nine ports under Rear Admiral Don P. Moon on U.S.S. *Bayfield* from Plymouth. 110 vessels left from Plymouth carrying U.S. VII Corps of the 4th Infantry Division. These were among the first troops to land on Utah beach.

The second wave was made up of the 29th Infantry Division planned to land on Utah beach on the second high tide. Led by U.S. Commander C. D. Edgar, B Force comprised in total of seven divisions made up of 25,000 men with 4,429 landing vehicles departing from various ports.

Plymouth was after D Day the main replenishing port for U.S.N. bombardment ships off the coast of France then by late June, July and August a receiving base for troops displaced in the fighting and in need of rest and reallocation to other units. Some 6,000 of these passed through Vicarage Road camp during these months.

As a foothold was secured in Europe and Allied Forces moved across France the need for the base at Plymouth and others along the coast declined. In August, 1945, a decommissioning officer was appointed to bring matters to an end and in September the various locations around this area were closed so bringing to an end another episode in the history of this city.

Acknowledgements

I am greatly indebted to many people and organisations for giving of their time and effort in answering my letters of enquiry, allowing me to interview them and for loaning photographs many of which have been reproduced in this publication.

Most of the contents of this title came from sources in the United States of America and I record my many thanks to the U.S. Army Military Institute, U.S. Navy Records Department, Dr. E. Eckstam, Wisconsin, G. Frederick, Montana, and Manny Rubins, Plymouth. Much closer to hand are Lt. Com. D. Spencer, U.S.N., Crispin Gill, P. Richards, G. Barker, Mr. and Mrs. McDonald and those listed with quotations from their experiences in this area in 1944. I was also able to use the resources of the *Western Morning News* archives, the Plymouth library and the West Devon Records Library. I hope that this small publication may recall at least some of the memories of those now far off days when peace was still an uncertain goal.

Arthur L. Clamp,
203 Elburton Road,
Plymouth, Devon PL9 8HX

Senior Military Commanders in Plymouth

General Dwight D. Eisenhower, Supreme Commander of Allied Forces with Major General Charles Gerhardt and Air Marshal Sir Arthur Tedder, are watching a demonstration during an inspection visit to the American 29th Infantry Division on 4th February 1944. The exact location is not known.

U.S. NAVAL ADVANCED AMPHIBIOUS BASE, PLYMOUTH, ENGLAND

On 8 November 1943, the U.S. Naval Advanced Amphibious Base, Plymouth, was commissioned. The Commanding Officer was Capt. C. F. M. S. Quinby, U.S.N., and the Executive Officer was Comdr. W. G. Hurlbert, U.S.N.R. Headquarters of the Commanding Officer was located at Hamoaze House, Mount Wise, Devonport.

The 29th and 81st U.S. Naval Construction Battalions engaged in extensive building programs, and two months after formal commissioning all facilities were fully functioning and operational. Maintenance and repair departments were located at *Queen Anne's Battery*, with Lt. Comdr. Charles L. Pierce, U.S.N.R., as Officer in Charge; *Saltash*, on the Tamar River, with Lieut. John F. Deery, U.S.N.R., as Officer in Charge; and *Calstock*, further up the Tamar River, with Lieut. F. Walcutt, U.S.N.R., as Officer in Charge.

The original engineering force consisted of 18 officers and 278 enlisted men. From the date of the first engine change to the present time, USNAAB, Plymouth, has serviced a total of 3,000 craft, 897 of them having been drydocked. An aggregate of 14,788 individual jobs was completed, ranging from minor items to major hull and machinery repairs on all types of craft. This work ranged from the conversion of two 4,200-ton British cruisers, to repair jobs on all types of landing craft and transports, DE's, DD's and BB's.

The major repair activity of the Plymouth command comprised what is known as *Queen Anne's Battery* which is fully equipped with shipfitter shop, blacksmith shop, propeller repair shop, carpenter shop, paint locker, bosn's locker, machine shop, engine repair and overhaul shop, optical shop, radio material shop and electrical shop. Three wharves and docks, together with three marine railways for the handling of LCI(L)'s, LCT's, LCM's, and LCV's, were in use at all times. Considerable additional work was done at the Royal Naval Dockyard, Devonport, in which we had the use of two drydocks almost continuously. Two floating drydocks, capable of lifting 400 tons, have been recently built and have been in daily use since.

Saltash and *Calstock* were repair sub-bases servicing small craft and YMS's. Hull repairs, engine repairs, billeting, and supplying of all craft were done at these bases. *Vicarage Road Camp*, with Lieut. C. W. Carr, U.S.N.R., as Officer in Charge, billeted more than 2,000 enlisted men and 175 officers, with *Shapter's Field* billeting approximately 1,700 men and 200 officers.

The U.S. Naval Dispensary, *Manadon Field*, was opened on 12 February 1944, with the Senior Medical Officer being Comdr. F. J. Weddell, Jr., (MC), U.S.N. Originally designed as a 100 bed unit, this dispensary was enlarged to 245 beds, and in the event of emergency these beds could be replaced by doubledeckers and the dispensary made a 500 bed unit. The dispensary is unique in that it is entirely a hut camp consisting of 61 huts built into an integral unit.

The Work before Invasion

This, then, was the physical set-up of the sub-bases which made up the USNAAB, Plymouth, but a description of it is far from giving an adequate picture of its functioning, which became more and more important as the hour for invasion approached. *Queen Anne's Battery*, for example, soon found that in addition to work on landing craft, it was capable of sending repair parties aboard ships in the harbor, warships and transports. Personnel from this sub-base were loaned to the British Admiralty upon occasion and worked in the Royal Naval Dockyard. Marine railways, originally planned for LCI(L)'s and LCT's, were also used for hauling out SC's and YMS's and small Army tugs. A portion of the Rhino ferries and other floating equipment used in the invasion were built by the 1006th Construction Battalion at Plymouth. These CB's also participated at Cattedown Wharf in the unloading of ships and stores for the large supply base at Exeter.

The two large receiving stations, *Shapter's Field* and *Vicarage Road Camp*, in addition to performing their primary function, developed comprehensive programs of instruction in seamanship, signalling, aircraft recognition and first-aid. Furthermore, each of these sub-bases furnished numerous working parties daily where and as needed by the base as a whole.

Unquestionably the most important job, extraneous to the original function of the various sub-bases, was the organization of hard parties for the loading of invasion craft prior to and during the early stages of the invasion. The loading during practice invasions and landings synchronized the entire effort so that the final loading proceeded without a flaw. All available officers and enlisted men of the base turned to in a concerted effort to keep the steady stream of LST's, LCI(L)'s, and LCT's flowing smoothly, together with the loading of transports with a shuttle service of LCVP's. This was a 24-hour a day task, and approximately 36,000 men and 60,892 tons of equipment and supplies were loaded across Navy hards from D minus 14 to D plus 14.

In like manner, the officers and enlisted men of the dispensary had the task of inspecting and furnishing medical aid and supplies to all Navy ships in the area, maintaining first-aid stations on all hards on a 24 hour bases, while the dispensary itself was also in the constant condition of emergency readiness.

During the operation of the base, the operations of all U.S. Navy vessels in this vicinity have been carried on by USNAAB, Plymouth, through Commander-in-Chief, Plymouth R.N.

Liberty Ship, 7,000 tons

These very large vessels carried most of the military equipment and personnel from the States to various ports in the U.K. The photograph shows Landing Craft Tanks being loaded in Devonport Dockyard sometime after the Normandy Landings.

After the Invasion

With the assault and build-up phases of the invasion safely passed into history, USNAAB, Plymouth, could afford to look upon its first great mission as satisfactorily completed, but that did not mean any great relaxation. Hard parties were no longer necessary, but a constant stream of traffic, men and vessels soon began to pour in from the far shore. USNAAB, Plymouth, maintained a 24 hour workday for the repairs, maintenance, and supply of all U.S. Naval forces afloat. *Vicarage Road Camp* was converted into a survivors' camp for the clothing, outfitting, and rehabilitation of returned personnel from the ships afloat and the shores of Normandy. After D-day though, there was a little more time for some of the amenities; serious efforts were made to beautify the grounds around the hut camps, galleys and laundries were enlarged and improved, and an attractive officers' lounge was installed at *Shapter's Field*. Leaves and liberties, impossible to grant before the invasion, were reinstated. *Saltash* and *Vicarage* operated with greatly reduced personnel, and *Calstock* closed completely. The numerous hards were returned to the British along with some temporary docking facilities.

On 10 June 1944, Capt. Newcomb L. Damon, U.S.N., assumed command of this base, relieving Capt. Quinby, who was ordered to Portland, Weymouth, to serve as Commanding Officer of the U.S. Navy base there.

On 13 July Comdr. Hurlbert, Executive Officer, died at *Manadon Field* after an operation and prolonged illness. Lieut. Robert G. Lockton, U.S.N.R., who had assumed Comdr. Hurlbert's duties during the latter's illness, carried on in the post until relieved by Lt. Comdr. Robert A. Brown, U.S.N.R., on 20 July.

Although Plymouth sustained two air raids and five alerts during the operation of the base, no damage or injury was suffered by U.S. Navy personnel or property.

On 5 January Rear Admiral Alan G. Kirk and Rear Admiral John S. Wilkes made an inspection of the base, and on 25 February, Admiral Harold R. Stark, COMNAVEU, made an informal inspection.

U.S. Naval Amphibious Receiving Base, Plymouth — St. Budeaux

On 24 July 1944 the hut camp at *Vicarage Barracks*, overlooking the Tamar River opposite Saltash, was set up as a separate command, the U.S. Naval Amphibious Receiving Base, Plymouth, under the command of Lieut. C. W. Carr, U.S.N.R. It has served as a billeting and messing center for transient officers and enlisted men, an extremely important service since the movement of craft and men to and from France began. Housing, food and medical facilities for the large number of personnel accommodated have been adequate, although at times the housing situation has been tight.

Recreation facilities, however, an important matter in a base where men have temporarily little to do, have at times been inadequate, particularly in light of the very limited facilities offered in Plymouth other than "pubs". For that reason this activity, since its inception, has provided regular recreation in the form of dances, reading room, library, movies and sports facilities. In consequence, it believes, it has possibly eliminated additional problems in the town.

Official U.S. Report on its Plymouth Base.

Queen Anne's Battery Dry Dock

Pontoons are being repaired here which was part of an extensive engineering programme for maintaining many kinds of craft including Army tugs, coastguard vessels and even captured German vessels. It was almost a 24 hour schedule of work preparing for the 6th June, 1944; damaged vessels were repaired as well after the landings.

Shapter's Field

The exit to this camp, not far from Queen Anne's Battery, where vehicles were maintained and a variety of domestic work took place such as the laundry, barber's shop, etc. The 97th Construction Battalion was stationed here.

Names were not supplied with this group photograph, they were simply described as one of the many "operations" gang maintaining equipment and looking after supplies.

The "Wet" Canteen

This is one way of describing a bar where military personnel can get a drink but not quite in the English style. The adapted nissen hut is at Shapter's Field where off duty hours can be spent talking about the day's work or about home.

The Post Office
Each main camp in the Plymouth area had its own mailing facilities with the main mail post being somewhere in the Barbican. Here mail from home could be collected or sent most of it being flown out from Harrowbeer to a central depot in the U.K.

Ship's Store
Outside view of the laundry and tailoring nissen huts presumably where the three pictures were taken of the work inside. This is still at Shapter's Field and gives some idea of the extensive facilities provided at this camp.

Shapter's Field 1946
It is August and the camera records locked nissen huts and a job well done in housing and preparing troops for the June 1944 landings. They have all gone some, perhaps, to the States and it will not be long before these huts are demolished and a chapter closed on the use of this part of the city.

The Laundry

This was run by First Class P.O. W. A. Ackerman in 1944 with twenty-five men under him at Shapter's Field camp. In one month's work 419 blankets, 10,870 lbs of sheets, tablecloths, etc. and 3,037 bundles of personal clothing were handled.

Ironing Room

Another of Shapter's Field nissen huts was given over as an ironing room an important facility when uniforms had to be pressed for special parades. It is not known if men did their own ironing or whether Shapter's Field was the centre for this work for the whole Plymouth area.

Trouser Pressing

This may be taking place in the same nissen hut as the ironing and it looks as if personnel are waiting for their uniforms to be finished. The large trouser press on the right labelled *American* no doubt could cope with the continuing demand from local servicemen.

Workshop Activities

Handling stores, making sure that each unit has sufficient to keep going and maintaining large stores placed in various quarries and open spaces around Plymouth was part of the battalion's work as seen here. Cutting wood for hut building, fencing, barge construction and a host of other uses together with engine servicing and electrical routine work made up much of the day for these men working on many locations around the city.

Feeding the Five Thousand

The food and stores requirements for so many servicemen stationed in the Plymouth area meant that battalions of men had more than enough to do just to keep this large amphibious advance base going from day to day without giving too much thought about the actual invasion preparations themselves. One of the many cook houses is shown below.

Sea Bees

This affectionate title was given to the numerous Construction Battalions who set up the various camps around this area and then concentrated on a wide range of maintenance and later repair work to hundreds of vessels engaged in the assault on France.

Three views of the workshop activities show men keeping abreast of demands for mechanical and electrical servicing to jeeps, station wagons, a variety of landing craft, cars, security measures for the many ammunition dumps scattered around Plymouth and the housing and domestic needs for thousands of personnel based here. Many of these men were also directly engaged on constructing barges, dry docks and the very large Rhino ferries.

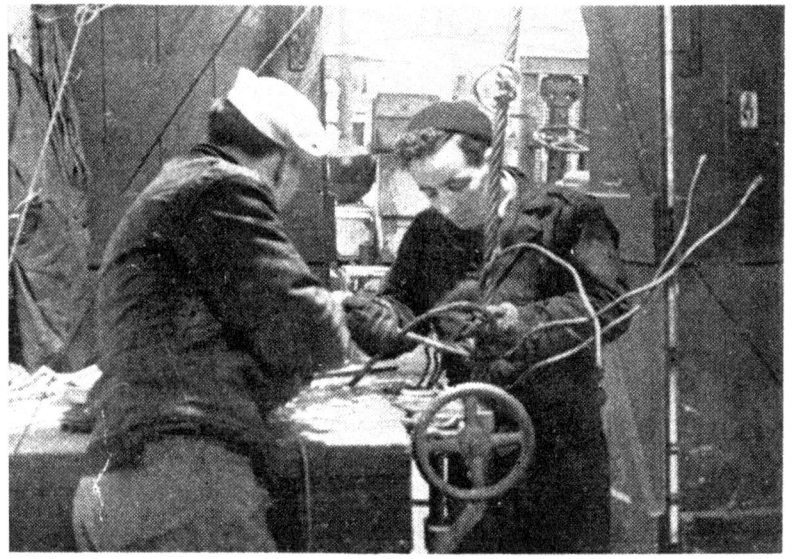

U.S. TROOP LOCATIONS AROUND PLYMOUTH

The U.S. Advanced Amphibious Base had various locations in the Plymouth area; in addition to these there were many others used by troops assembling in this marshalling area a few weeks before the Normandy Landings.

In fact, almost any open area was taken over and temporary accommodation set up often in tents, huts or houses and buildings in which the briefings for the landings took place. The following locations make up the Amphibious Base and the majority of troop locations during May and June, 1944, but it is very likely there were many more required for holding the 36,000 personnel who left from Plymouth in the eventful days of June, 1944.

Amphibious Base Locations

Queen Anne's Battery: This was in use from November, 1943, to September, 1945, and was the headquarters of the Base. It occupied the waterfront and part of Teat's Hill Flats in which was the communications centre for the Plymouth area. The Construction Battalions built a ship repair yard, dry dock and three marine rail tracks to repair and service a variety of craft.

Shapter's Field: This nissen encampment provided a wide range of domestic services such as footwear repairs, laundry, barber's shop and a chaplain's office. The 97th Construction Battalion was here with accommodation for 1,100 officers and men. Mechanics serviced jeeps and other vehicles here as well and in all about 5,000 transient personnel passed through its gates. Lt. Com. G. A. Moneysmith was officer commanding assisted by Lt. Com. W. B. McColl.

Fleet Post Office: This was in the Barbican handling all the mail for the Base. Some 121,000 incoming sacks were received and 125,000 were outgoing under the supervision of Lt. J. A. Watts, postal officer.

Martin's Wharf: This was just below Laira Bridge and occupied part of the waterfront by the former power station. The officer in charge was Lt. J. W. Kimble; Landing Craft (Mechanical) were moored in rows and acted as marine taxis providing a ship to shore service.

Cattedown and Pomphlett Quarries: These were used for storing equipment and materials some of it in warehouses erected by the CBs. *Cattedown wharf, Cole's, Elliott's* and *Laira yards* were also used as storage depots.

Commercial and Baltic Wharfs: The waterfront below Madeira Road was taken over as repair slips for Landing Craft Vehicle and Personnel; nissen huts were erected as workshops and this unit worked closely with the larger unit at Queen Anne's Battery.

Turnchapel Hards: Concrete block platforms were laid down at Sycamore Beach over which Landing Ship Tanks were loaded with assault vessels and personnel. This was one of the main embarkation points in the area.

Victoria Wharf: Another ship repair unit with supply and engineering huts that worked closely with QAB.

Richmond Walk Wharf: Known as *Commando Way* (the walk had a large board painted with *Idaho Way*) maintenance work on craft took place here and then it was used as a loading hard for Landing Ship Tanks.

Manadon Field Hospital: It was opened on 12th February, 1944, closed on 31st August, 1945, and built to handle the expected intake of casualties from France as well as providing medical care for the thousands of U.S. troops stationed in this area. It was under the charge of Commander K. R. Weston and had an X-ray, dental, surgical, orthopaedic, traumatic and ear, nose and throat departments. Equipped with 250 beds it was planned to double this number if large numbers of casualties resulted from the landings.

Vicarage Road Camp: This large camp at St. Budeaux was opened in January, 1944, and closed in September, 1945, through which about 60,000 troops passed many on their way to Normandy from the hards at Saltash Passage. It was first used as a records camp keeping accounts of all personnel pay, etc. with a complement of 10 officers and 225 men. After the landings it acted as a reception centre for men returning from Normandy handling about 6,000 survivors who were kitted out and then sent on to other units.

Saltash sub-base: This was set up for servicing small craft and minesweepers just below the rail bridge in November, 1943. Lt. Com. T. H. Harris was in charge throughout its use closing on 31st August, 1945. Here LCI, LCT and PT flotillas were maintained.

Central Park Stores: A large warehouse was erected here to hold meat with other buildings to store food and general provisions for the area. Its records show that it provisioned 3,177 craft including cigarettes and clothing.

Construction Battalion camps: Camps had to be set up to accommodate the large influx of engineers, etc. to construct the bases around Plymouth's waters. Camps were sited at *Efford* (*Little America* takes its name from this period), *Calstock, Ivybridge* and *Saltash*.

Barnpool Hards: Another embarkation point which was built by the 110th Field Artillery which did their training in the park. Troops of the 29th Infantry Division, who were mainly sited in Cornwall, left from here.

Nissen Huts

The huts are situated on the site wh the Royal Sailors' Rest stood in F Street in the heart of busy Devonp In the 1940s coloured American tro lived in these huts that stretched r down Catherine Street. Barclay's B is on the corner of King Street. Sc Devonport people remember the band concerts held by the Uni States Forces in Fore Street.

Marshalling area Locations

The enormous build up of troops and military equipment in the Plymouth marshalling area meant that many kinds of permanent and temporary facilities had to be set up to ensure the smooth flow of personnel and resources in readiness for the landings in France. Among these were:

American Red Cross Club: This was at Elliot Terrace occupying five of the houses providing refreshments and recreational outlets for white personnel stationed in the area. Accommodation was also available and it was manned by civilians.

American Red Cross Club: This second club was for the coloured troops and was in St. James Terrace behind the Hoe. It was opened from March, 1944, and closed in September, 1945.

U.S. Shore Patrol H.Q.: This was in the old Stonehouse police station in East Street from which patrols kept a watchful eye on the behaviour of troops and the maintenance of order when personnel were off duty.

Saltash Passage Hards: This was the main embarkation point for U.S. troops who had been accommodated in Vicarage Road camp, St. Budeaux, and around the Plymouth area. Extensive concrete hards were built here and there is a memorial standing to this period with the road down which they march called *Normandy Way*.

Devonport Dockyard: Dry docking facilities were made available to U.S. forces where they built two floating docks.

Saltram House Grounds: This was taken over as a massive parking area for hundreds of vehicles standing under camouflage. There were also nissen huts in the grounds and the area was heavily guarded.

Hamoaze House, Mount Wise: The headquarters of the U.S. Naval service under the command of Captain C. F. Quinby, U.S.N. Three more commanders served here until its closure in September, 1945.

Edinburgh Street Camp, Devonport: Set up to accommodate Rear Admiral D. Moon and his staff in order to be near Hamoaze House.

Coypool at Marsh Mills: Coded depot G75 it held extensive stores under the command of Col. Higbee; officers lived in the nearby Gables House and other ranks lived in nissen huts built along Forder Valley Road.

Other locations: Chaddlewood tented encampment, *Dunstone Road*, Plymstock, where cooking facilities were set up. *Raglan Barracks* and the *Brickfields* used for parking dozens of ambulances close to tented accommodation, *Devonport Park*, and the bottom of *Fore Street*, the last for coloured troops. *H.M.S. Raleigh* at Torpoint, *Plaisterdown Camp*, Tavistock, used by the wounded back from Normandy in the large hospital and *Brixton* village.

During the build up in March, April and May, 1944, many sites around Plymouth were simply requisitioned and adapted for marshalling purposes prior to leaving for the assault on Europe.

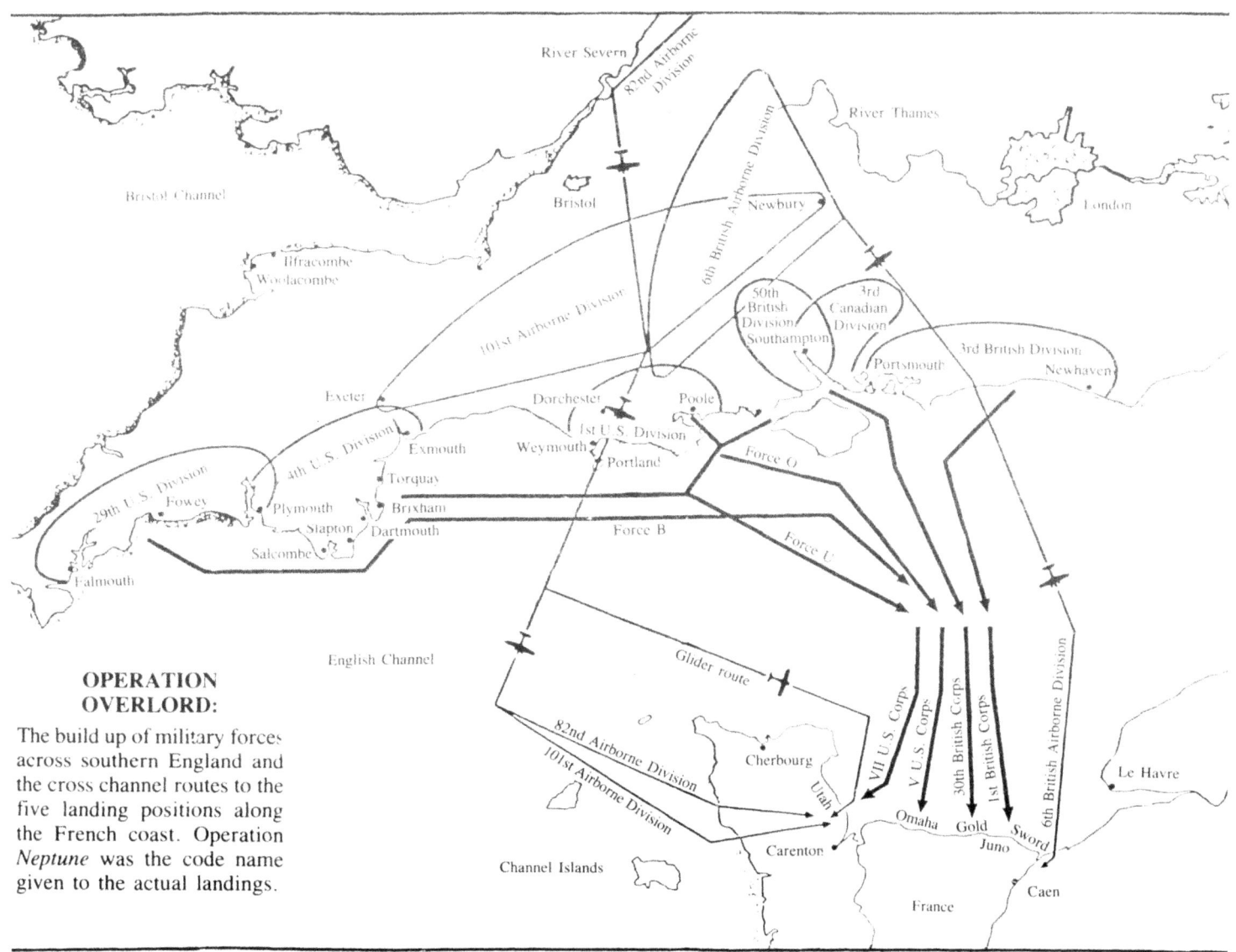

OPERATION OVERLORD:

The build up of military forces across southern England and the cross channel routes to the five landing positions along the French coast. Operation *Neptune* was the code name given to the actual landings.

Cattedown Wharf
Large steel pontoons are being put together by U.S. Construction Battalions seen here. They were used as landing platforms in deep water off the French coast when Landing Ship Tanks could not get in close to the shore.

Landing Craft Mechanised
Moored on the Hamoaze loading is taking place in readiness for the invasion. Alongside are US 580, Landing Craft Utility, and LKA 8, Assault Cargo ship, sometime in the Spring 1944.

Turnchapel Hard
The concrete and wire mesh hards were laid down to facilitate the movement of tanks and heavy vehicles across soft tidal land as seen here. Turnchapel was one of the embarkation points around Plymouth; a Landing Ship Tank is about to take on vehicles for the sea crossing to Normandy. Note the former power station in the background at Prince Rock.

Commercial and Baltic Wharves

Repair slips for Landing Craft Vehicles and Personnel were constructed here occupying the water frontage up to Madeira Road. The three rather poor photographs on this page show part of the work taking place and in the top scene the old entrance to Sutton Harbour can be identified. Nissen huts were the workshops, a crane was used to bring craft up the slipway and repair work was accordingly done. The work here was linked to the much larger operations taking place on the opposite bank at Queen Anne's Battery.

Some of this work continued after the D Day landings when damaged craft returned to Plymouth for repair and return to the battle zones along the French coast.

Martin's Wharf

There were rows of LCMs, Landing Craft Mechanical, moored here for use around Plymouth for moving stores, going out to liberty ships, etc. It was referred to as a *seagoing parking lot*. The crews lived in huts along the wharf with their own mess hall. Top left shows one of the boat crews; above is a compass crew under Lt. W. W. Shinners and, left, stands Lt. J. W. Kimble, officer in charge and W.O. W. Moody.

Saltash Amphibious Training Base

This was set up in November, 1943, to service and repair Landing Craft Infantry, Landing Craft Tanks and other vessels along part of the waterfront below the rail bridge. It came under the command of Lt. Cdr. T. H. Morris from its beginning until its decommission in April, 1945. Personnel were accommodated in nissen huts and from various reports the U.S. servicemen were well received by the local people and quickly integrated with the social life of Saltash.

Manadon Field Hospital

This was opened on 12th February, 1944, to provide extensive medical facilities for U.S. servicemen serving here and on the front to be opened in France in June, 1944. A brief report states that it was built in two months and stands on rubble from the blitzed areas of the city. All the medical equipment, beds, etc. were brought in from the States.

£500 U.S. Gift To P.O.W. Hospital

A CHEQUE for £500 was presented to the Prince of Wales's Hospital this morning on behalf of U.S. naval officers and men of the Advanced Amphibious Base, Plymouth.

The presentation at the base headquarters was made to a hospital delegation headed by Mr. C. P. Brown, chairman of the Board of Management.

The occasion marked the formal retirement of Capt. N. L. Damon, as commanding officer of the base. Capt. Damon, who has been ill for several weeks, got up from his sick bed specially for the occasion.

In his address, Capt. Damon said: "We Americans owe a debt of gratitude to the people of the City of Plymouth which we can never fully repay. Help and friendship have been given to us here during the year in which I have been in command, and as a token of appreciation the officers and men of this base present this cheque to be used in helping to restore some of the damage caused by the ravages of this war."

In reply Mr. Brown remarked that the hospital staff had been only too happy to help them in any way possible, and were very touched by such a gracious tribute. The money is to be used to equip a dental clinic.

Sunday Services

A nissen hut could quickly be adapted as a church for service especially when large numbers of personnel were stationed in the area for only a short time. The stress and strain building up to the landings must have often turned the thoughts of men to their maker and in the quietness of a service make peace with Him.

LOCAL REPORTS OF U.S. TROOPS ACTIVITIES

March 1943: Americans erected two large nissen huts as social centres, one at the beginning of **Manadon Hill** and the other at Victoria Road, St. Budeaux. Dances and refreshments are offered. On one occasion an 11 year old girl sang at a dance and £100 was raised towards her going to a singing school.

March 1943: American troops in the Palace Theatre subscribed £27 towards the musical education of a 13 year Devonport girl, Patricia Thomas, who sang an impromptu song during the interval of an ENSA concert.

June 1943: An American softball team will play against a Canadian firefighters' team at Plymouth.

June 1943: American army truck drivers are being taught the English highway code by a British policeman. Accidents occur and U.S. trucks are often too wide for Devon's roads.

July 1943: A large number of U.S. officers attended a reception in the Abbey Hall given by the Lord and Lady Mayoress of Plymouth. There was also a dance in the lecture hall. American army nurses, Wrens, WAAF and ATS joined with many Americans in the evening's programme.

August 1943: Americans' Gift to Hospital. Members of the U.S. Army made a collection for the Prince of Wales hospital. The amount was £9 8s. 0d.

September 1943: Sgt. Gay of the Plymouth Civil Defence Service is teaching Americans the details of British firefighting.

October 1943: Leading citizens of Plymouth, heads of services were amongst those present at the Palace Theatre to hear Roland Hayes the famous American negro tenor and a choir of twenty-four American negro soldiers.

December 1943: Hundreds of children in Devon and Cornwall, including Plymouth, are to have the time of their lives at Christmas as guests of the U.S. Army. Huge trucks will take hundreds of children to monster parties throughout the two counties.

December 1943: Four parties with 350 to 400 children in each took place in Plymouth organised by local U.S. troops. £500 was raised from one American ship in the Sound towards the costs.

December 1943: Miss Margaret Clarke's pony *Bambi* was knocked down by a jeep and her hind leg was broken. Four departments of the U.S. Army helped in putting it in splints and the pony is now on the road to recovery.

December 1943: A big childrens' party will be given by the American Red Cross in Elliott Terrace on the Tuesday after Christmas. Troops are already dropping in offerings in a box labelled "Save your candy for childrens' party". Children of the volunteer staff and 50 poor children will be invited.

January 1944: U.S. servicemen were guests at the Octagon Youth Club, Stonehouse, on Friday night. Members put on a pantomime *The Old Lady who lived in a Shoe* which was much appreciated by the troops.

January 1944: Visitors to the Merchant Navy Week exhibition in the Plymouth Art Gallery had the chance of handling an American Lewis gun.

January 1944: The opening of the U.S. Red Cross Club in Elliott Terrace was made by Mr. Harvey Gibson of the American Red Cross Commission. There are now 125 such clubs in the U.K. and it is managed by Mrs. Massey assisted by Miss Johnson.

January 1944: American artillerymen with red piped khaki hats and members of the W.R.N.S. formed a guard of honour outside St. Matthias Church, Plymouth, for the wedding of Corporal James Bower, U.S. Army, from Virginia and P.O. Patricia Ross, W.R.N.S., of Norton Avenue, Plymouth.

February 1944: American soldiers who were farmers in the States made a tour of farms in Devon recently visiting Totnes, Kingsbridge and South Brent areas.

March 1944: After their successful tour in the Middle East the *Sky Blazers*, the U.S. 9th Air Force's famous entertainment unit, will appear in the Palace Theatre, Plymouth, to entertain local U.S. troops. A group of singers, dancers and a comedian will make up most of the two part programme.

April 1944: At Emmanuel Church, Plymouth, yesterday 1st Lieut. John R. Davidson, from Houston, Texas, was married to Miss Betty P. King of Gifford Place, Mutley.

April 1944: Books for U.S. Navy. The *Western Morning News* has appealed to its readers for books, especially novels and detective stories, for American sailors stationed in Plymouth. They should be sent to Marlborough House, Marlborough Street and marked "For United States Servicemen".

May 1944: Eighty people paid half a crown each to hear one of America's well known pianists play at Emmanuel Church Hall on Thursday evening. Sgt. Hans Heidemann of New York, U.S. Army, will be giving more concerts in this area.

May 1944: Entertainment by the U.S. Air Force. The Palace Theatre will be closed to the public but open free to all members of Allied Forces this week. It has been lent to the Special Service section of the 8th U.S. Air Force for their musical show *Skirts*. Lieut. Arthur Brest with an all male cast of fifty will give the show. Tickets are available at the American Red Cross Club.

May 1944: A Plymouth girl, arriving at the barracks at Crownhill to say Goodbye, found the gates locked; the men were confined to quarters, awaiting embarkation, but eagerly shook hands, like prisoners, through the bars.

June 1944: A Plymouth girl, arriving for work in the Home Guard office at the Docks at 9 a.m. looked down at hundreds of GIs boarding boats and knew they were bound for France. My heart ached. I could hardly see for tears. Other girls hurried to the Hoe to find that the vast armada of craft recently assembled there had vanished in the night (3rd June).

July 1944: A dance will be held on the Hoe on Tuesday evening between 7 and 9 p.m. arranged by the Lady Mayoress as an Independence Day event for American forces. Music will be provided by an American Dance Band.

October 1944: Lieut. S. Piazza, U.S. Army, was married to Miss Frances Jordan, a Land Army girl, at Plympton St. Maurice yesterday.

November 1944: Private 1st class William Klopher, U.S. Army, and his brother Frank, U.S. Navy, met in Plymouth last week for the first time in 3 years.

American Red Cross Club

This was opened in January, 1944, by Mr. Harvey Gibson, American Red Cross Commissioner in Elliott Terrace to provide accommodation, refreshments and recreational facilities for white U.S. troops. Mrs. Massey was superintendent and at the opening Lady Astor was presented with flowers by P.O. E. B. Wilson, U.S. Army.

Seen here are Sally Jackson, Betty Stemler and Marge Hauke standing in front of an American Red Cross Club mobile canteen given by the people of Detroit. This would go around the area to the various troop locations supplying light refreshments.

Dances were also held here at least once a week with a band from Denbury.

Beryl Postlethwaite

This 1944 dated identification card gives more details of the American Red Cross at Elliot Terrace supported by civilian staff drawn from local people. Below is *Rough* an American on duty in the club but no more details are given about him.

Coloured American Troops Club

An American Red Cross Club for coloured personnel was opened at 3 and 4 St. James Terrace, Plymouth, in March, 1944. Mr. Corneff Taylor was in charge assisted by Miss Geneva Holmes and it was staffed by U.S. troops. There were 65 beds, canteen and recreational facilities for locally serving troops.

This closed in September, 1945, when there were twenty-six volunteers under Mrs. H. W. Banks. Mrs. E. Ackroyd was manageress, Leonard Mann, chef; Albena Ferris, Dorothy Isgrove, Muriel White, Gladys Brierly, Katherine Cook, L. Warner, Miss W. Pooley and Miss Butina Paget were among those who received certificates in recognition of their services.

U.S. Navy Shore Patrol
Of all the U.S. personnel serving in Plymouth the white-capped truncheon carrying special patrol (Navy police) will best be remembered for their smartness of uniform and alertness to trouble. The headquarters building is St. George's Hall, East Street, Stonehouse, used after the war by Royal Navy Shore patrols up to the 1950s.

Stand by Your Jeeps!
These small fast vehicles criss crossed the city on patrol and could soon be on the scene of any trouble which did occur from time to time among service personnel. With thousands of U.S. personnel on duty in the Plymouth area and many others passing through on their way to France special patrols had more than enough on their hands.

Air Support for D Day
It is September, 1943, and an American pilot has been posted to Bolt Head to gain operational experience with R.A.F. personnel for air cover duties over France during the weeks leading up to June, 1944.

SOME PERSONAL RECOLLECTIONS

W. Glover, Plympton: I was about twelve or thirteen and I was able to get a regular supply of American comics from the U.S. Navy Shore Patrol H.Q. in Stonehouse which in those days were like gold dust. The comics changed hands until they were in tatters. Having access to new ones made me a comic baron!

C. Stokes, St. Budeaux: We saw many American drunken sailors going down to the cells in George Place after a night out in Union Street; the MPs used to give us lads chewing gum!

J. Curno, Southway: We used to talk to the U.S. Navy patrols and in their quieter moments we handled and aimed the little *Garand* rifle which they carried. It was small, like a toy, and was easy for us boys to lift. It was carried in the jeeps and kept in a special holster attached to the vehicle. We also spoke to the prisoners in the *Brig* as they called the jail in Stonehouse.

M. May, Beacon Park: The U.S. Navy took almost every spare piece of coastline in the Plymouth area; Stonehouse Pool, Richmond Walk, Mount Wise and they had a huge camp in Fore Street, Devonport. With the large number of ships in the Dockyard and the mecca of Union Street for the run ashore the siting of Patrol H.Q. in Stonehouse made good sense.

Mary Outhwaite, Turnchapel: We lived along the main road in Hooe and when the *ducks*, (I believe that was the name taken from their initials DUKWS), passed our house en route to Turnchapel and the landing craft we would stand in the garden or at the window and wave at the troops. Without exception they would wave back very often throwing us sweets, cigarettes and sometimes money. How upset my mother was when a large carton of cigarettes thrown at us landed in next door's garden. They were non-smokers, but the carton made good bartering material. One incident remains very clear in my mind. Among the thousands of troops we must have waved off there was one lad with bright carroty red hair. His cap was off and his hair was blowing madly about. That picture of him is so clear and I often wonder what happened to him. My mother used to feel rather embarrassed when walking me around to Turnchapel via Barton Road as on several occasions the road was lined with G.I.'s who wolf whistled her.

D. Steer, Dover: My journey to work took me past Plympton St. Mary, Underwood, Stag Lodge and down Colesdown Hill. As I cycled daily changes were taking place to the area. I saw the pill boxes being built and then during 1944 the roads around Stag Lodge were dug up and concrete laid down. Within weeks areas of trees were cut down behind the Lodge, part of Saltram Estate of Earl Morley. Soon the grounds were full of Americans and a mass of military vehicles of all shapes and sizes was accommodated there. There was always an armed guard on duty at the various Saltram Lodges.

K. Bullard, Milehouse: As boys we could walk around the city quite freely. I remember seeing the American tents in Home Park where the white troops were accommodated and down at the Brickfields we watched baseball and softball being played behind the camp perimeter. It was here that over 100 ambulances were parked in readiness for the landings and as children we would say, *Touch your nose, touch your toes, never go in one of those.*

Special Pass while at Vicarage Road Camp

Survivors from the Slapton tragedy at this camp were issued with special passes identifying them as bona fide U.S. officers while walking around Plymouth. The U.S. Shore Patrol police would have otherwise taken them in because of their casual clothing and having no official documentation as to their rank or unit.

```
U.S. NAVAL ADVANCED AMPHIBIOUS BASE
   VICARAGE RECEIVING BARRACKS,
        Plymouth, Devon.
                                    ENCL
                              ----------------
                                   (Date)

From:    Officer in Charge
To:      Shore Patrol

Subject: Special Liberty to Survivors

    1.   In accordance with verbal instructions given to me this
man, _____, Serial No. _____ has
been granted the privilege of taking liberty without being in the
uniform of the day because: (Check one)
                    ( ) a. He is a survivor and is unable to
                           comply with the uniform regulations
                           due to the inability to draw clothing
                           of the proper size.
                    ( ) b. His status is such that he is not
                           entitled to draw clothing at this
                           time

    2.   He is cautioned not to abuse the privilege.


                              C. W. Carr
                              Lieut. U.S.N.R.
```

Survivors from Slapton at Vicarage Road Camp

Dressed in fatigues but carrying the small insignia of an officer these men survived the German E boat attack during an exercise in April, 1944. They are Alexander Brown, Tom Clark, Fred Beattie, Ed Panter, M.D., James Murdock, Gene Eckstam, M.D., Bernard Carey, Doug Harlander and "Scoffy" Gill. They were later taken to Exeter for new uniforms and then re-allocated to different units in readiness for D Day.

U.S. Jazz Band Heads March Past

This is on the occasion of a *Salute the Soldier* week in 1944; the parade is watched by civic dignitaries on the right close to the damaged Guildhall.

Salute the Soldier Week

Allied Forces often joined in march pasts for these war fund raising weeks as seen here in May, 1944. Two U.S. Army personnel flank two U.S. Navy men carrying flags at the head of their column. Note the tower of St. Andrew's church just in the background.

Normandy Hill

This name plate commemorates one of the routes taken by the marching soldiers from Vicarage Road Camp down to the hards at Saltash Passage. The troops came down to this marshalling area from Taunton and passed along here on 2nd and 3rd June, 1944, in readiness for embarkation to France.

Vicarage Road Camp at St. Budeaux

A close but rather poor view of the camp itself which housed about 2,000 U.S. personnel. It was set up in January, 1944, mainly acting as an accommodation base and instruction centre for troops in training for the Normandy Landings.

Saltash Passage Memorial

The granite columns come from ruins in Plymouth holding the plaque which records the departure from here of the V and VII Corps of the United States Army for the Utah beach landings on 6th June, 1944. Nearby were concrete hards and a slipway covering about 5,000 square yards and extending 200 feet into the water.

Aerial view of St. Budeaux showing Vicarage Road Camp in 1945

Although this photograph was taken just after the war the nissen huts can be clearly seen to the right of the rail bridge and just below it part of the American built hards still stand in the water. U.S. troops also occupied the old stables at St. Budeaux wharf while on the Saltash side there was a sub-base servicing minesweepers and small craft. Vicarage Road Camp was decommissioned on 25th August, 1945.

Raglan Barracks, Independence Day, 1945

This is 4th July and it is celebrated by U.S. Forces stationed in this country as seen here in Devonport. The garrison commander is addressing troops in what looks like a downpour of rain judging by how the men are dressed.

Edinburgh Road Camp, Devonport

This was recorded being built in ten days on blitzed ground in Fore Street for accommodating Rear Admiral D. Moon's staff who had just been drafted to Plymouth from Africa in the Spring 1944. He was the commander of Group 2, 11th Amphibious Force. The camp had offices, wardroom's, recreation and mess halls and was close to Hamoaze House where the Rear Admiral was involved in planning. He was first offered accommodation on the U.S.S. battleship *Bayfield* then moored in Plymouth waters but turned this down.

Richmond Wharf

A close view of one of the many light tug boats operated by the 329 Harbour Craft Company doing duty all around the Sound in moving large vessels in and out of port. The date is 20th March, 1944.

Richmond Wharf

A 30 ton crane is brought alongside a U.S.S. battleship transferring heavy equipment or materials. This type of crane would work in various locations around the Sound also assisting in heavy maintenance work. The date is 20th March, 1944: the crane is operated by the 329th Harbour Craft Company.

Unloading Landing Ship Tanks

LSTs 283 and 44 are moored somewhere on the Hamoaze. Presumably they have just arrived from the States and the 30 ton crane is unloading equipment from them. It is the 20th March, 1944, and the work is undertakened by the 329 Harbour Craft Company.

Barge Construction

Personnel of the 329th Harbour Craft Company are at work on the Cornwall side of the Hamoaze assembling barges from prefabricated units. The date is 20th March, 1944, and work is taking place almost round the clock for the build up to the landings of 6th June, 1944.

Briefing for D Day Landings, 26th May, 1944

Commanders from all units in the Plymouth area assemble in the Odeon cinema for a briefing on the assault plans for Normandy given by General B. Montgomery a matter of days before the departure from Plymouth late May, 1944.

Lending a Hand

The date is 16th November, 1943, and U.S. troops are helping in salvaging furniture and belongings from properties damaged in yet another raid on the city. This was one of many similar responses shown by allied forces stationed in Plymouth throughout the war.

```
Viscount and Lady Astor                              10 July. 1945.
3 Elliott Terrace
The Hoe Plymouth.

Dear Lord & Lady Astor,
            For nearly two years the City of Plymouth has been
a gracious host to the U.S. Army.  I believe, a detachment of the
14th Port who arrived in July 43 was the first "permanent" installation.
Since then, Plymouth has seen the ranks of the "Yanks" and "Rebels"
swell to many thousands.  Now however, we are shortly due to leave.
The American Army will be with you no longer.
                                Sincerely.
                                D.H. Black.
                            D.H. BLACK. MAJOR TC USA.
```

American troops helping in clearing up work in 1944 after a raid.

Welcome to American Troops
Arrangements for Independence Day celebrations

Friday, 2nd July 1943: Dance for enlisted Americans accommodated in the two gymnasiums at Plumer Barracks, Crownhill. Colonel Canham is in charge and will be issuing invitations to the American servicemen and to members of the WRNS, ATS, WAAF and Sisters from Plaister Down Camp hospital, Tavistock. The dance will be from 8 to 11 p.m.

Saturday, 3rd July 1943: Reception for 150 American officers at Abbey Hall. The Union Jack and Stars and Stripes will drape behind the platform. A band will be playing. 3.30 to 5 p.m.

Saturday, 3rd July 1943: Dance for 150 American officers in the Lecture Hall, Plymouth Guildhall. Band of the Royal Marines will play. The following have been invited to send groups of lady officers: WRNS, ATS, WAAF, Plaister Down and Royal Naval hospital sisters, Red Cross and St. John's Ambulance VADs. 8 to 11 p.m. Twenty young civilian ladies will also be invited. Mrs. Colin Campbell will choose girls who regularly attend officers' dances.

Sunday, 4th July 1943: There will be an open air service next to the Naval Memorial led by the U.S. chaplain, W. F. Burke. The memorial will be draped with the Union Jack and Stars and Stripes flags. 3.15 p.m.

American Anti-aircraft Gun

The continuing bombing on Plymouth prompted allied forces to engage their own men and guns in the defence of the city. The cleared blitzed area provides a temporary platform for this gun to operate against the background of Charles Church sometime in 1944.

"Wings for Victory" Parade

There were a variety of parades throughout the war as part of many special week's fund raising for the war effort. More often than not service personnel stationed in the area would take part in the event as seen here with American soldiers marching in front of the city museum sometime in 1944.

Salvaging Homes

Help again is given and the use of a large truck made for taking away the contents of houses damaged in a raid. Much of it was placed in stores from where owners could retrieve items when alternative accommodation became available. The date is 16th November, 1943.

St. Andrew's Church

As part of the Independence Day activities in July, 1943, in Plymouth, Admiral of the Fleet, Sir Charles Forbes and Lady Forbes, show two senior American Army officers around the blitzed building.

Bulldozing Rubble

The aftermath of any large raid meant that a lot of clearing up was necessary; roads had to be cleared and dangerous buildings demolished. Here Americans lend a hand with heavy machinery to assist in these tasks.

Loading Landing Ship Tanks at Barnpool

A closer view of the intensive activity is captured in this photograph showing troops of the U.S. 29th Infantry Division in line for going aboard L.S.T. 496. L.S.T. 51 is alongside and in the background is the old grain store at Millbay. Note the *hards* or concrete block platform laid over the beach to carry heavy vehicles such as these *Weasels*, cargo carriers M-29s.

Loading L.S.T.s at Barn Pool, Mt. Edgcumbe

125 mm Howitzer guns are going aboard the Landing Ship Tanks on probably 3rd June, 1944. Troops are from the 29th Infantry Division having driven from the Bodmin area and other locations in Cornwall. General Omar Bradley spoke to all the servicemen from a jeep prior to departing for Normandy.

Landing Craft Infantry leave for Normandy

The date is either the 2nd or 3rd June, 1944, and five LCIs are seen here loaded with infantrymen leaving Plymouth for the last time setting course up channel to join other U.S. craft leaving from various West Country ports. LCI 325, LCI 321 and LCI 250 can be identified.

U.S. Military Abbreviations

RCT: Regimental Combat Teams
DE: Destroyer
LCV: Landing Craft Vehicles
SC: Sub chaser
YMS: Yard Minesweeper
CB: Construction Battalion
LCVP: Landing Craft Vehicle and Personnel
LST: Landing Ship Tank
LCV: Landing Craft Vehicle
LCM: Landing Craft Mechanical
GI: Government Issue

PC: Patrol Craft
LCA: Landing Craft Assault
LCI: Landing Craft Infantry
BLT: Battalion Landing Team
LCT(R): Landing Craft Tank (Rocket)
PC: Patrol Craft
PT: Private
BUCO: Build up Control
LSI(H): Landing Ship Infantry (Headquarters)
GSK: General Stores

Great Generosity to Plymouth Children

WE announced last week that the American troops in the Westcountry intend to give Devon and Cornwall kiddies a royal time during the Christmas.

The U.S. Navy has now chimed in.

The American sailor is not going to let his knaki compatriots get away with it like that. No, sir!

A Ship's £500

The Lady Mayoress (Lady Astor) has received a generous gift of money from the crew of a United States ship "to use as she thinks best for Plymouth kiddies."

This sum represents the larger part of £500 raised by the officers and men of the ship.

One of the officers said that although the men had families of their own and commitments at home, they had been so struck—and they have been in action themselves—by the way Plymouth was carrying on that they have "really stinted themselves" to give all they could to make this a happy Christmas for the people of the city.

Part of the money has been distributed to orphanages and other institutions which can use it in a Christmassy way for young and old folk.

A Hundred Hosts

Lady Astor's suggestion was a party, and a great show is to be held on Wednesday in Virginia House, when a hundred of the American sailor hosts will be present. Although it will be a children's party essentially, representatives of the different clubs attached to Virginia House will be invited as well.

Good for the Navy!

Meanwhile the U.S. Army is keeping the competition not with one of the "hottest" items in nickle, the supply of a "rare delicacy" to the young guests (Can this mean ice-cream?)

"A Real Beano"

There are to be four "mammoth" parties, each for 350-500 children—two to-day, one to-morrow, and one on Tuesday.

The Americans intend a real beano, and are giving up not only their own sweet rations, but also sweets which have been sent to them from the folks at home, for the delectation of Plymouth children lucky enough to get an invitation.

The children will go to the parties in groups, under the direction of their own teachers, and have a U.S. soldier assigned to each group as guide and general putter-on to good things. These good things include entertainments, rides in jeeps, and a Father Christmas.

All this seasonal good-will, be it noted, is being provided by the troops. No "official" money is being spent.

A Red Cross Party

Another big children's party will be given by the American Red Cross in Elliot Terrace on the Tuesday following Christmas. Already American troops are dropping handsome offerings into a box which says, "Save your candy for the children's party."

Lady Astor has been invited to attend, and guests will include 50 poor children, as well as the children of all voluntary workers attached to the Amerian Red Cross in Plymouth.

What Americans Buy in Plymouth

AMERICANS visiting Plymouth have experienced difficulty in buying souvenirs to take home, but shop assistants find them cheerful customers and on the whole easy to please.

Among the first things they make for are view cards, now becoming very scarce. Many have shown their interest in trying to see as much as possible of this part of the world by searching for maps of Plymouth and Devonshire, both of which are difficult to obtain.

Maps of Plymouth can only be bought on the production of a police permit.

Cosmetics—and Books

Clothing and sweet rationing, of course, limits their range, and the shops have only a small variety of fancy goods to offer. For their wives and sweethearts at home (or may be their English girl friend) they have picked mainly on cosmetics, handbags and flowers.

In the bookshops their choices have been confined chiefly to travel and literature on the Westcountry, plus a few novels.

At the Stationers'

Notepaper for writing home is an essential and from the stationers they have also bought box-files, drawing instruments and rubber stamps.

The china and glassware they have purchased is apparently for use in the messes. None of the hand painted china and pottery Americans were so fond of before the war is being made now.

One shop reports a run on photo frames.

A Peach at 2/6

Two American visitors who entered a fruiterer's shop on Matley Plain saw some peaches for sale and told the shopkeeper they were the first they had seen since leaving their own country. They would like to have bought one—but decided that 2s. 6d. was "a bit dear."

Pigeons' D-Day Work

JUST before D-Day and for several days after many Plymouth people were puzzled to see American jeeps stopping at frequent intervals outside some houses in the City in whose back-yards were pigeon lofts.

During the early days of the landings jeeps and soldier pigeoneers, fully armed, constantly patrolled the lofts of members of the Plymouth Group of the National Pigeon Service who had undertaken to supply the American 1st Army with birds for D-Day operations.

Actual preparations started many months before. Members were sworn to secrecy and placed under a security measure section of the U.S.A. Signals Pigeon Company. Constant touch was maintained between them and Mr. H. C. Woodman, pigeon supply officer for the district, and the birds were given daily operational training by the U.S. Army Pigeon Section on a coast-line some 100 miles long in Devon and Cornwall.

In Honour of U.S. Sailors at Plymouth

Party at Virginia House

IN appreciation of the £500 which a United States ship has provided for the Xmas entertainment of Plymouth children, a large party of ratings was entertained at Virginia House Settlement on Wednesday evening.

They had an opportunity of hearing some of the tiny tots sing carols, and later junior girls executed some tap dances and sang songs with an American flavour in honour of the guests.

The main part of the programme was a dance in which those over 18 were able to participate as well as some of the mothers of the nursery group. Altogether there are about 1,000 members of the Settlement, but as they could not all be accommodated to meet the generous American sailors, representatives of all the groups were invited.

For the dance, music was provided by Hyde Park Centre Band, and Mr. Fred Cavendish was M.C. Lady Astor, Lady Mayoress of Plymouth, arrived early in the evening, and after encouraging the Nursery Children in their singing by distributing sweets with the aid of some of the sailors, joined wholeheartedly in the dancing.

Newspaper Articles

Although there were many restrictions on reporting some articles passed the censor as these four relate events of 1943 and 1944 involving U.S. troops in Plymouth.

Arthur L. Clamp – the man behind the books

Arthur Leslie Clamp was a man of boundless energy with a passion for helping others, particularly through his love of history. A printer by trade, he started his career in a printing company before moving his family from Exeter to Plymouth to teach at the Plymouth College of Art and Design, where he eventually became the Head of the Printing Department.

Arthur with his five children.

A Devoted Family Man

Despite his love of teaching, Arthur prioritised his family, always making it home by 5:30pm for tea. He and his wife, Rosemary, raised five children: Susan, Angela, Elizabeth, David, and Steven. Arthur would often combine his love of family and history by taking his children on Sunday walks, encouraging them to appreciate historical monuments by taking photos or making crayon rubbings of gravestones for his books. The family home at 203 Elburton Road was a hub of activity, with a large garden, featuring a two-storey fort and a makeshift swimming pool.

A Lifelong Learner and Adventurer

Arthur's thirst for knowledge extended beyond history to a deep curiosity about the world. He was passionate about exploring different cultures, traditions, and cuisines, often taking advantage of his long summer holidays as a teacher to travel to places like India, Russia, South America, the middle east and the USA, sometimes bringing one of his children along. This adventurous spirit even influenced his home life, as seen by the short-lived family tradition of steam-cooking vegetables after a trip to Iceland.

History is a prominent feature of family days out

Community and Philanthropic Spirit

His commitment to serving others was evident in his long-standing involvement with the Elburton Methodist Church. He was the Sunday School Superintendent for over 15 years and served as the editor of the wider church's monthly newsletter, "The Link," for a similar duration. After Rosemary's very sad passing, Arthur later remarried and, following a chance encounter with a professor from India, established a connection with a missionary school in Chennai. Together with his new wife, Christine, he co-founded a "Sponsor a Child's Education" program that continues to this day.

*Pictured left – The cover of 'The Link' complete
with hand drawn sketches of each church by Angela
Below right – Arthur Clamp promoting his latest book
Below left – Arthur at home with his first wife, Rosemary
Below centre – Arthur on holiday with his second wife,
Christine*

A Legacy of Learning and Positivity

Arthur's greatest passion was history, which he brought to life through tireless research, documentation, and the many books he authored. He was driven by a need to "never be stuck in a rut," constantly seeking new experiences, meeting new people, and expanding his knowledge. With a positive attitude and a great sense of humour, he was always ready to help others, leaving a lasting impact on his family and community. His children, Susan, Angela, Elizabeth, David, and Steven, remember him with love and gratitude.

David Clamp, 2025

A Legacy of Local History

Below is the story of how Arthur L Clamp began writing books, in his own words, drafted shortly before he passed away in 2001. I have only made minor alterations to this text, correcting grammatical errors that he did not survive to correct himself. When I first discovered this text, I was shocked to see my name mentioned. It seems that, unbeknownst to me, I shared my first PC with him. I suspect he used it during the day when I was at school, although I do have one memory of sitting with him and showing him how it worked. It has been a pleasure to pick up where he left off and see his books republished and redistributed, and to know that I was part of the story, even back then. It was also fascinating to discover that his pricing structure matches the way I have tried to price the books, with a third going to local sellers and the rest covering printing costs with a little left over for my expenses.

I am his eldest grandson, and it is a privilege to curate his legacy, which we are calling 'The Clamp Collection'. The very last line of the text originally reads "The following pages list all the titles." Sadly, that page is missing and we have no record of all the books he published and knowing that some of those were researched by other authors makes the process of finding them even harder. I look forward to one day completing the collection and seeing them all available again. And maybe, one day, I'll even start writing my own to add to the series. For now, here is his story in his own words.

Steven Gibson, 2025

Writing and Publishing Booklets on Local Topics and Areas

I started this interest in either 1968 or 1969 when living in Woodford. I had by these dates established the Department of Printing and I think I must have been looking for something different to do. The first titles were of A5 size proofed from type set at Clarke, Doble and Brendon, Ltd., Plymouth printers, and then made up into pages and printed at Sawtell and Neilson, Ltd., Totnes.

Then began a slow process of getting them out to shops, etc. which proved to be more time consuming and difficult than actually researching, writing and getting the books into print. However, I persisted and opened a business account with Barclays Bank on the Broadway. I was advised to give it a title so I called it "Westway Publications". There came along another problem, one of storage of paper and finished books which was solved when the family moved to Elburton in 1970.

I changed the printer to Penwell, Ltd., Callington, Cornwall, as he was then just setting up himself and his prices seemed very reasonable. I did not get any of the printers to make up the complete books. I hand folded the flat printed sheets, stitched the books on a small manual table stitcher and trimmed them in a small hand turned guillotine which I bought from someone in Penzance for £40. It was brought up in a van.

The trouble and time going to and fro to Callington was too much so I transferred the printing to PDS Printers, Prince Rock, Plymouth, and I have been with them ever since. Now they are at Plympton which is easy to reach and they fold the flat sheets which was turning out to be a long chore which only saved a small part of the printing costs.

All my first titles were written by myself. I took the photographs and developed them in the loft of the house, the type was set by now on a computer situated in the house at Elburton from which I had collected photographic lengths of text to cut up and law down as pages.

At some point I decided that I would do my own film processing of lith film so I bought a large second hand process camera from Kingsbridge and learnt through trial and error to make line negatives of the text and halftone negatives of the illustrations which proved more difficult than I anticipated. The main problem was trying to keep the developer in the large dish at the correct temperature as any change would affect the developing time. I replaced this old camera with a brand new one bought from Croydon, Surrey, costing £900. This has turned out to be a great asset cutting out an expensive part of the printer's costs and one crucial aspect of the work which I could control.

By the middle 1970s there were many outlets I had contacted in Plymouth, up to Dartmoor, Exeter, around to Torbay, Totnes, Dartmouth and the South Hams. The market for local books was much greater than I had first thought and through getting to know many local people undertaking research themselves had the chance to help and make up books for other people who had in most instances, got together a collection of photographs with some text in a rather muddled way. Through my experience in print I was able to shape up their work and get it into print and in every case I had to pay the printer and let the person have the royalties. In the majority of titles produced in this manner this was another way of producing titles and it did give some profit to my work. However, I must say that in a few cases I lost out by either the other person getting the numbers wrong, not returning any monies from stock I delivered or they thought that more of their books should have been sold.

The print run was usually 1,000 copies and from time to time I have had reprints of 250 copies. It took about ten years to clear the first print run so I always had large stocks in the garage, workshop, etc. The numbers sold during the early years was about 7,000 copies a year increasing to around 9,000 copies and for the whole of the enterprise about 500,000 have been sold. The booklets have become part of the local scene and many people collect them, shops regularly order copies and I go around certain areas month by month restocking or replacing titles as necessary.

During the past year or so I have started setting the text on a Packard Bell PC, something which I should have done some years back. I share it with Steven Gibson, my grandson. There appears to be no end to the market for local books, but I could not earn a regular income because of the long time it takes to sell stock.

However, now exceeding 100 titles made up mainly of A4 twenty-four page booklets, some folded guides, with selling prices set with a third going to the shop which is the trade custom, the original idea has been quite successful and could go on for ever.

Apart from monetary benefits, however spasmodically these might be, I have learnt a lot myself, met many interesting people and have become part of the local scene with requests to give talks and to advise people about getting into print.

Arthur L Clamp, 2001

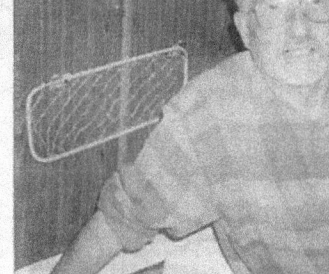

This newspaper article, published by the Evening Herald on 17th August 2001, forms a good record of his life. Just as he encourages us to learn more about local history, we encourage you to learn a little about him. For that reason, we have included these pages at the back of all the most recently republished books, in honour of his memory and recognition of his contribution to the community.